YOUNG SCIENTIST CONCEPTS & PROJECTS

THE SEA

ROBIN KERROD

Gareth Stevens Publishing
MILWAUKEE

The original publishers would like to thank the following
children, and their parents, for modeling in this book —
Emily Askew, Maria Bloodworth, Alistair Fulton, Sasha Howarth,
Alex Lindblom Smith, Sophie Lindblom Smith, Kerry Jane Morgan,
Jessica Moxley, Elen Rhys, and Joe Westbrook.

**For a free color catalog describing Gareth Stevens'
list of high-quality books and multimedia programs,
call 1-800-542-2595 (USA) or 1-800-461-9120 (Canada).
Gareth Stevens Publishing's Fax: (414) 225-0377.
See our catalog, too, on the World Wide Web: http://gsinc.com**

Library of Congress Cataloging-in-Publication Data

Kerrod, Robin.
The sea / by Robin Kerrod.
p. cm. — (Young scientist concepts and projects)
Includes bibliographical references and index.
Summary: Explores the ocean depths, sweeping tides and currents,
northern inlets, coral reefs, and other aspects of the waters of the
world; includes fact boxes and suggested experiments.
ISBN 0-8368-2164-5 (lib. bdg.)
1. Ocean—Juvenile literature. [1. Ocean.
2. Oceanography—Experiments. 3. Experiments.]
I. Title. II. Series.
GC21.5.K47 1998
551.46—dc21 98-4856

This North American edition first published in 1998 by
Gareth Stevens Publishing
1555 North RiverCenter Drive, Suite 201
Milwaukee, WI 53212 USA

Original edition © 1997 by Anness Publishing Limited.
First published in 1997 by Lorenz Books, an imprint of
Anness Publishing Inc., New York, New York.
This U.S edition © 1998 by Gareth Stevens, Inc.
Additional end matter © 1998 by Gareth Stevens, Inc.

Editors: Jenny Fry and Ros Carreck
Consultant: Bryan Bett
Photographer: John Freeman
Stylists: Marion Elliot and Melanie Williams
Designer: Caroline Grimshaw
Picture researcher: Liz Eddison
Illustrators: Stephen Sweet and John Whetton
Gareth Stevens series editor: Dorothy L. Gibbs
Editorial assistant: Diane Laska

Printed in the United States of America

1 2 3 4 5 6 7 8 9 02 01 00 99 98

THE SEA

CONTENTS

THE RESTLESS SEA

I F you were an alien visiting from space, you would see Earth as a blue planet with scattered brown patches. The vast areas colored blue are water, and the brown patches are land. Over seventy percent of Earth's surface is covered with water that forms a huge world sea, or ocean. If you tasted seawater, you would find it very salty, unlike the freshwater in rivers and lakes. The sea has many fascinating rhythms and ever-changing moods as the waves pound the shore and the tides flow in and out. It teems with a variety of life, from microscopic single-celled creatures to enormous whales weighing up to 150 tons (136 metric tons). You do not have to be an alien to discover the secrets of the sea. You can visit the seaside and find out for yourself how fascinating it can be.

During the summer months, many vacationers visit the seaside, where they sunbathe, swim, and sail.

In stormy weather, huge waves crash against the rocks, reminding us how powerful and dangerous the sea can be. The constant battering of the waves will, in time, break the toughest rocks into tiny pieces. This daily pounding also cuts into cliffs, creating caves and arches. Collapsed arches leave pillars of rock called stacks.

Heavyweights

A humpback whale and her calf cruise in their watery habitat. Blue whales are the largest creatures of the sea, weighing up to 150 tons (136 metric tons). They spend most of their time underwater, but, as mammals, they must surface to breathe.

On a coral reef in Indonesia, a grouper eats a long-nosed butterfly fish. These two kinds of fish are common on coral reefs around the world.

Sail and steam

In 1838, the *Great Western,* built by British engineer Isambard Kingdom Brunel, was the first steamship to provide regular service across the Atlantic Ocean. It sailed between Bristol, in south-western England, and New York, on the eastern coast of the United States. The ship was built of wood and powered by paddle wheels, but it had sails in case the engine failed.

AT THE SEASIDE

Most of us like to go to the seaside in summer to swim, to walk along the beach, or to play in the sand. The seashore is also a fascinating place to investigate. Something interesting is always happening as the waves crash down and the tide rolls in and out twice a day. Plenty of wildlife can be found in the water, in the air, on the beach, hidden under the sand, or in tidepools. One way to learn about these plants and animals is to examine a section of the shore. The projects on these two pages show you how. You can make an underwater viewer to help you see water creatures more easily. The viewer cuts down on reflections from the surface, which usually spoil your view. When you visit the seaside, be sure to take along some field guides to help you identify the plants and animals you see.

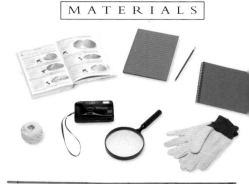

You will need: roll of string, bamboo canes, notebook, pencil, gloves, magnifying glass, camera, field guides.

Investigate the shore

1 At low tide, stretch some string from the edge of the water to the top of the beach. Use bamboo canes to hold it up. Walk along the string, writing down what you see.

2 At the top of the beach, you will find land plants that are able to live in a salty environment. Wear gloves and use a magnifying glass to examine these plants.

3 The high-water mark on shore, where seaweed, dead fish, and driftwood are left behind by high tides, is interesting, too. Seaweed flies and sandhoppers live there.

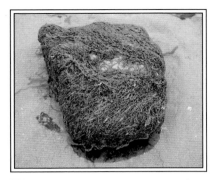

4 On the upper shore, you might find green seaweed clinging to exposed rocks. Use a camera to take pictures of it for your notebook.

5 Farther down, on the middle shore, you might find wide banks of brown seaweed, called wrack, and clusters of barnacles.

6 Other brown seaweed, called kelp, is often carried by incoming tide from the lowest part of the shore to the upper shore.

WARNING

Do not go near the sea alone and be careful when you walk on wet, slippery rocks. Watch out for the tide coming in and beware of fishing hooks, broken glass, and debris on the shore. Always wear gloves when handling shells and plants from the seashore.

Make an underwater viewer

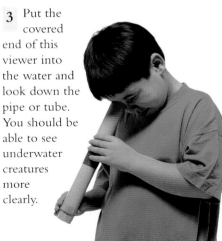

1 Cut out a circle of contact paper 1 inch (2.5 centimeters) larger in diameter than the pipe or tube. Peel off the backing on the sticky side.

2 Place the circle over the bottom of the pipe, pressing it down firmly around the edges. Put a rubber band around it for a watertight fit.

3 Put the covered end of this viewer into the water and look down the pipe or tube. You should be able to see underwater creatures more clearly.

SEA WORLD

Coral islands, such as this one (above) in the Pacific Ocean, are surrounded by reefs built by tiny sea creatures called polyps. Polyps deposit hard calcium cups around their soft bodies. When they die, other polyps build on the limy remains.

Ice cold

The Arctic Ocean is the smallest ocean in the world. It is almost surrounded by the landmasses of Europe, Asia, North America, and Greenland.

SEAWATER covers about seventy percent of Earth's surface. This vast area is divided into seven oceans, although it actually is one continuous body of water. There are five main oceans — Pacific, Atlantic, Indian, Arctic, and Antarctic, which is also called the Southern Ocean. The largest of these oceans, the Pacific and the Atlantic, are divided by the equator into northern and southern parts, which gives us seven oceans altogether. Sailors used to refer to them as the Seven Seas, but, even though the words *sea* and *ocean* are thought to mean the same thing, *sea* more accurately refers to a smaller body of water within a larger ocean. A sea is often partly enclosed by land, such as the North Sea between the British Isles and continental Europe.

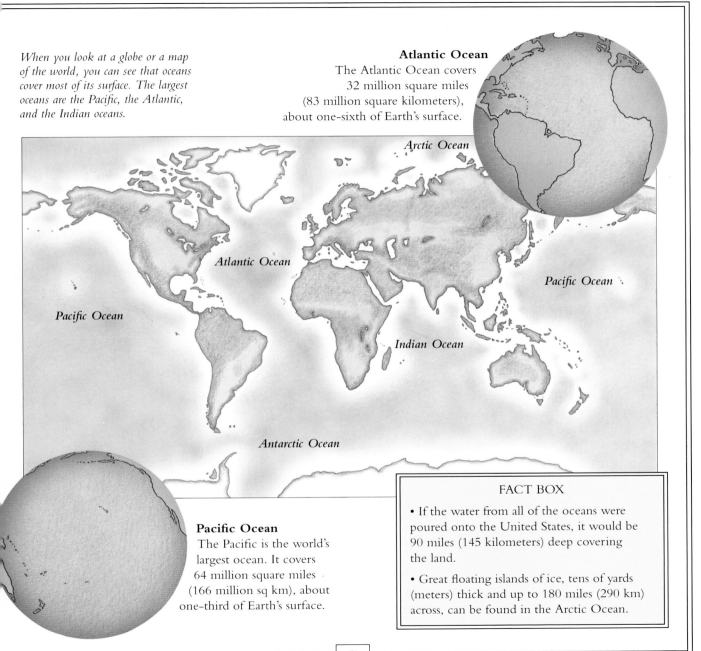

When you look at a globe or a map of the world, you can see that oceans cover most of its surface. The largest oceans are the Pacific, the Atlantic, and the Indian oceans.

Atlantic Ocean
The Atlantic Ocean covers 32 million square miles (83 million square kilometers), about one-sixth of Earth's surface.

Arctic Ocean

Atlantic Ocean

Pacific Ocean

Pacific Ocean

Indian Ocean

Antarctic Ocean

Pacific Ocean
The Pacific is the world's largest ocean. It covers 64 million square miles (166 million sq km), about one-third of Earth's surface.

FACT BOX

• If the water from all of the oceans were poured onto the United States, it would be 90 miles (145 kilometers) deep covering the land.

• Great floating islands of ice, tens of yards (meters) thick and up to 180 miles (290 km) across, can be found in the Arctic Ocean.

BIRTH OF THE SEAS

WHEN Earth began, some four and a half billion years ago, there were no oceans. It was extremely hot, so water existed only as vapor. When Earth started to cool down, the water vapor condensed into storm clouds, and rain fell. Eventually, water formed pools on Earth's surface, and, nearly one billion years later, oceans were born. The early oceans and continents were not in the same places they are today. They have been, and still are, moving. The crust that covers Earth is divided into plates like the six-sided shapes on a soccer ball. In some places beneath the oceans, the plates are moving apart, and the ocean floor is widening. In other places, the plates are moving together. When two plates meet, one slides underneath the other, dragging the seabed down into a deep ocean trench where it is destroyed in molten rock.

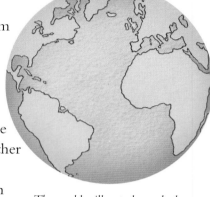

The world will not always look like it does today, because the continents are still moving.

200 million years ago

100 million years ago

50 million years ago

Drifting continents

About 200 million years ago, all of today's continents were combined in one great landmass called Pangaea. There was also one great world sea, known as Panthalassa. As the plates of Earth's crust started to move, Pangaea began to break up. The North Atlantic Ocean opened up first and slowly widened. About 100 million years ago, the South Atlantic began to grow as South America split apart from Africa. Fifty million years ago, South America and North America were separate landmasses. These two continents joined only about five million years ago.

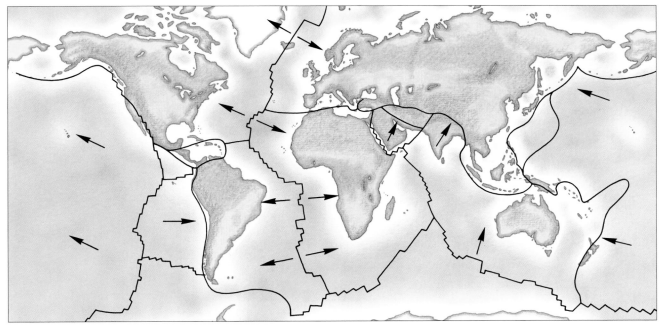

The moving plates

This map of the world *(above)* shows how Earth's crust is split into thirteen huge pieces, called plates. These plates are drifting together and moving apart very slowly. The arrows show the directions in which the plates are moving.

This map (right) *shows the northern end of the Red Sea, which separates Africa from Arabia. A boundary between two plates runs through the middle of the Red Sea. One plate is carrying Arabia eastward.*

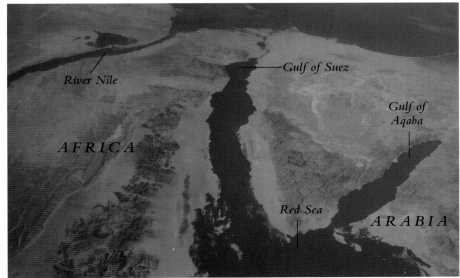

River Nile

Gulf of Suez

Gulf of Aqaba

AFRICA

Red Sea

ARABIA

DRIFTING CONTINENTS

THE rocky plates that form Earth's crust and carry the continents and the seafloor are always moving. In many places, the plates slide smoothly past one another. Sometimes, however, they jam and then, suddenly, jerk free, which creates earthquakes. Elsewhere, plates are colliding, and the pressure causes Earth's surface to wrinkle, forming fold mountains. The Andes mountain range in South America was formed, and is still changing, because a plate under the Pacific Ocean is colliding with the South American plate. In the middle of the Atlantic Ocean, a different kind of plate movement is taking place. The plate carrying North America is moving away from the plate carrying Europe, causing the Atlantic Ocean to get wider year by year.

Colliding plates
Sandwich together layers of modeling clay and push at each end to see how colliding plates create fold mountains.

A continental jigsaw

You will need: atlas, tracing paper, pencil, tape, colored cardboard, scissors.

1 Find the continents of North and South America, Europe, and Africa in an atlas. Outline the shapes of these continents on tracing paper.

2 Tape the tracing paper onto different colored sheets of cardboard and carefully cut around the outlines of the continents.

3 Place the eastern (right-hand) coasts of North and South America next to the western (left-hand) coasts of Europe and Africa.

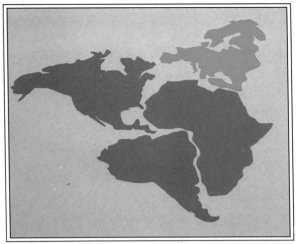

4 You will find that the coastlines of the Americas, Europe, and Africa fit together very well. Many scientists believe that these continents used to be joined together this way.

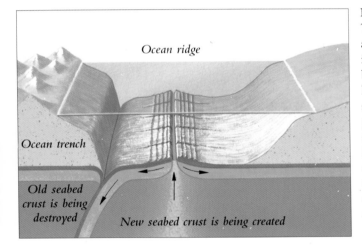

Ocean ridge

Ocean trench

Old seabed crust is being destroyed

New seabed crust is being created

The plates of Earth's crust are moving slowly over the hot, soft rock that lies beneath them. In some places, such as the Mid-Atlantic Ridge, the plates are moving apart, and molten rock is rising to plug the gap, forming new seabed rocks. In other places, one plate slides underneath another, forming an ocean trench. This process, called subduction, can create volcanoes or earthquakes.

Plates on the move

The continents of the Americas, Europe, and Africa sit on plates that are moving in opposite directions. Use the cardboard continents you made to see how they drift apart. Fold a large sheet of paper in half and attach paper clips along the fold. Tape the Americas on one side and Europe and Africa on the other. Drape the paper over two boxes. Push upward on the fold to see the continents move apart.

UNDERWATER LANDSCAPE

You might think the seafloor is flat and featureless, but you would be wrong. Deep down on the seabed are vast flat plains, great ranges of mountains, and deep valleys, called trenches or deeps. The tallest mountains and deepest valleys on Earth are found under the sea. There are also great fractures, or gashes, and many volcanoes.

At the edges of the continents, the oceans form a shallow region called the continental shelf. At the outer edge of the shelf, the seabed gently drops down to the ocean floor.

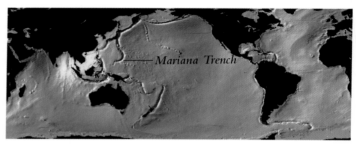

Seeing the seabed
The world's deepest waters are in the Mariana Trench. Satellites are used to help plot great trenches on the ocean floor.

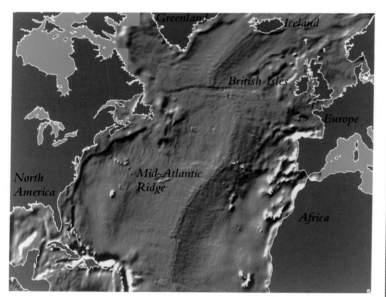

New seabed is being created along the crest of the Mid-Atlantic Ridge. It moves away to each side as molten rock rises from below.

FACT BOX

• Under the oceans, Earth's crust is, on average, 6 miles (10 km) thick, about a quarter as thick as the continental crust.

• The Mid-Atlantic Ridge is part of a 31,000-mile (50,000-km) mountain range.

• Close to mid-ocean ridges, the seafloor has holes, or vents. Liquids and gases containing minerals stream out of these vents from the hot rocks beneath. The vents are called smokers because of the smokelike effect produced when the hot minerals mix with the cold seawater.

• Metal-rich chunks, called manganese nodules, are scattered over parts of the Pacific Ocean's floor.

Submarine wonders

In the amazing landscape on the floor of the Atlantic Ocean, the most dominant feature is the *S*-shaped Mid-Atlantic Ridge, where new seafloor is being created from beneath. This ridge marks the boundary between crustal plates moving eastward and westward. Other features of the seafloor include vast flat plain regions, isolated seamounts, and mountains that stick out of the water as islands.

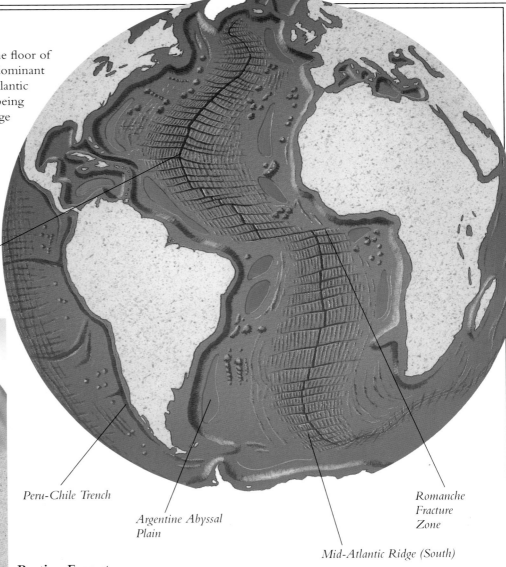

Mid-Atlantic Ridge (North)

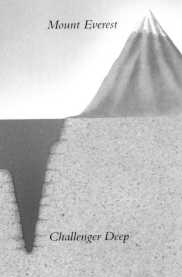

Mount Everest

Challenger Deep

Peru-Chile Trench

Argentine Abyssal Plain

Mid-Atlantic Ridge (South)

Romanche Fracture Zone

Beating Everest

Mount Everest, soaring to 29,028 feet (8,848 m) above sea level, is the world's highest mountain on land. The deepest point in the sea is Challenger Deep, in the Pacific Ocean, which descends to 36,200 feet (11,034 m).

THE SALTY SEA

SEAWATER is very salty and not good to drink because it contains dissolved minerals, or salts. The salinity, or saltiness, of the water is about 3.5 percent, although it varies from place to place. The main salt is sodium chloride, which is common salt, like table salt. There are also varying amounts of magnesium, potassium, and calcium salts and sulfates. The main source of these salts is rivers. As rivers flow over rocks on land, they slowly dissolve the rocks' minerals and carry them into the sea. Some lakes are salty for the same reason — the largest ones are called "seas," such as the Dead Sea. The salinity of seawater stays about the same because the water cycle keeps the amount of water in the sea more or less constant.

Swimmers float easily in the Dead Sea because there is so much salt dissolved in the water.

Water

Salt

Sodium chloride

Calcium

Sulfate

Potassium

Magnesium

These pie charts show both the amount of salts in seawater and the main substances in these salts.

This beautiful mineral is called a desert rose because of its roselike shape. It is a crystalline form of gypsum, a common mineral found dissolved in seawater.

Salty crust
A thick salty crust covers this salt lake *(left)* in the Tirari Desert of South Australia. Salt remained after the lake water evaporated in the sun's heat.

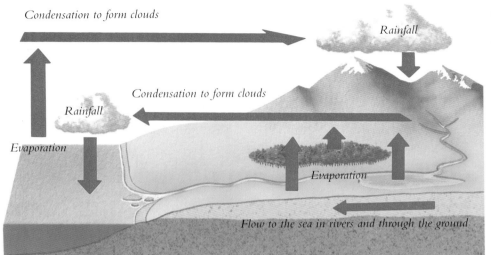

Condensation to form clouds

Rainfall

Condensation to form clouds

Rainfall

Evaporation

Evaporation

Flow to the sea in rivers and through the ground

Circulating water

The amount of water in the sea stays about the same because of the water cycle. The cycle begins when the sun evaporates water from the sea into vapor in the air. As vapor rises and cools, it condenses, or turns back into water in the form of tiny droplets. The droplets gather together as clouds and fall as rain or snow. The water eventually makes its way back to the sea in rivers.

Underwater oxygen

Some fish live in freshwater; some live in the sea. Very few fish, however, can live in both freshwater and seawater. Like humans, fish need oxygen, but they take it in through gills, rather than lungs. Both freshwater and seawater dissolve oxygen from the air. Water enters a fish's mouth and passes over its gills, which take the oxygen out of water the same way human lungs take the oxygen out of air. The water passes out through gill slits.

SALTY WATERS

*You will need:
measuring cup, large glass
container, scales, salt, spoon.*

O N our planet, there are trillions of tons of seawater. The project on this page shows how to make some more! The water you make will not be exactly like real seawater, but it will be very close to it, because the table salt you will use is the same chemical compound (sodium chloride) as the main salt found in seawater. The project on the opposite page shows how to make a hydrometer to measure the density of water. The word *hydrometer* means "water measurer." Seawater is more dense than freshwater because of the amount of salt dissolved in it. The higher the density of the water, the "thicker" the water is and the more easily it can support an object floating in it. You will find that the hydrometer you make sinks lower in tap water than it does in your "seawater."

Make some seawater

1 Carefully measure 3½ cups (840 milliliters) of water and pour the water into a large glass container.

2 Little by little, stir in 1½ ounces (42 grams), or approximately 2 tablespoons, of table salt into the water in the glass container.

3 When all the salt is dissolved, find out what seawater tastes like, more or less, by sipping a little of the water from a spoon.

You will need: scissors, drinking straw, modeling clay, glass container, tap water, pencil.

Make a hydrometer

1 To make a hydrometer, cut a drinking straw in half, roll a small amount of modeling clay into a ball, and push the clay onto one end of the straw.

2 Put the hydrometer into a glass container filled with tap water. Adjust the amount of modeling clay so the hydrometer just floats. Mark the water line on the straw.

3 Then put the hydrometer in the seawater you made. Look at the water line on the straw. You will find that it is lower than the one you marked before because seawater is more dense than tap water.

Plimsoll marks
Plimsoll marks are a series of lines on the side of a ship showing how low the ship, when it is loaded, can safely sink in certain water conditions. The top marking is *TF*, which stands for Tropical Freshwater. It is the top marking because the ship will sink lower in warm freshwater because of its lower density.

WAVES AND CURRENTS

THE sea is never still. Waves are constantly moving over its surface. They are set in motion mainly by wind — the stronger the wind, the higher the waves. Waves can travel thousands of miles (km) across the oceans. On the open sea, they ripple across the surface as they travel, but the water itself does not move forward with them. Near shore, water at the bottom of a wave drags on the seabed, and the crest, or high point of the wave, crashes onto the shore. Huge tidal waves, called tsunamis, are triggered by earthquakes on the seabed. In places, the water in the ocean moves in huge streams called currents. Currents can be hot or cold, and they have a noticeable effect on the climate. Most surface currents are caused by wind, but deep-water currents are caused by differences in temperature and density.

A surfer successfully rides an enormous breaker, or breaking wave.

Battering seas
This house is collapsing into the sea on the eastern coast of England. When the house was built, it was some distance from the sea, but, since then, the constant battering of waves has washed the cliffs away.

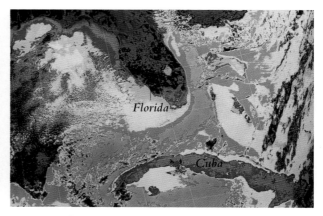

Currents from Space
Satellites can spot warm and cold currents in the oceans. This satellite image shows the warm Gulf Stream current (pinkish beige) flowing north past Florida.

El Niño's effects

This bush fire in Australia was caused by the effects of the El Niño current. The El Niño is a sea current that moves across the Pacific Ocean. Every few years, the winds weaken over the Pacific and the El Niño current reverses its direction. Such a change has a dramatic impact on weather conditions over wide areas, causing, for example, severe drought or flooding.

World currents

This diagram shows the main warm and cold currents that circulate around the world. The direction of the currents is affected by the shape of the ocean and the spinning of Earth. Notice how currents circle clockwise north of the equator and counterclockwise south of it. Currents move large bands of water through the oceans. They also affect the climate of the land they pass by.

Cold current ⟶   *Warm current* ⟶

MAKING WAVES

T HE projects on these two pages take a closer look at waves and currents and investigate how they are produced. We know that wind causes both waves and currents in water, but some of the purest waves can be seen when raindrops fall into a pond. Waves spread out in a series of perfect circles from the point where the raindrop enters the water. If you look carefully, you will see that only the waves move forward, not the water itself. Waves travel across the surface of liquids. The water itself moves only up and down as the wave passes through it. You can confirm this in the experiment with floats on the next page. The floats bob up and down, but they do not move forward. The experiment with the rope shows what happens. The rope does not move forward as the wave ripples along it.

Wind and waves
Fill a tank with water and blow across the surface. The surface ripples, forming tiny waves. The same thing happens to the sea when the wind blows across its surface.

Ever-increasing circles
When you drop a ball of modeling clay into water, it creates waves. The waves travel in circles away from the point where the clay entered the water.

Raindrop ripples
Raindrops make circular ripples when they fall on water. The ripples grow larger, but the water itself does not move outward.

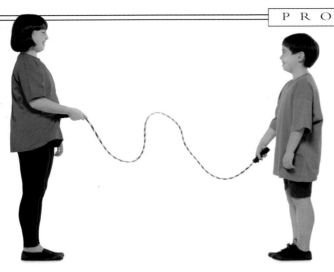

Bobbing up and down

Place some small floats in a tank of water. Hit the water at one end to make waves. Watch how the floats bob up and down but do not move forward as the waves travel across the surface of the water.

A wavy rope

Ask a friend to hold one end of a rope while you hold the other end. Let the rope sag. Then, quickly flick your end up and down. A wave moves forward along the rope. The rope itself moves only up and down.

Wind, waves, and currents

Sprinkle colored powdered paint on water in a tank. Blow gently across the surface and watch the paint move. Air moving over the surface of the water sets up currents the same way currents are produced at sea.

Wave approaches cork

Cork stays in position

Wave travels, cork does not

Wave motion

These diagrams *(above)* show a wave moving across water, while an object floating in the water moves hardly at all.

THE TIDES

I N most parts of the world, ocean waters gradually rise and fall twice a day. These movements are called tides. When the water is rising, the tide is flowing. When the water is falling, the tide is ebbing. Tides are caused by the gravitational pull of the sun and the moon and by Earth's spinning. As the moon circles Earth, it pulls at the ocean water directly beneath it, causing the water to rise. A similar rise in sea level occurs on the opposite side of the world, where the water bulges out as a result of Earth's rotating. Both places have high tide. About six hours later, the moon has moved on, pulling the water with it. The ocean has fallen to its lowest point, called low tide. How much the tide rises and falls depends on the alignment of the sun and the moon with Earth. The tide comes in farther and goes out farther on a spring tide; the range is not nearly as great on a neap tide.

Magic Moon
Although the moon is a small body, it still has enough gravity to pull water in Earth's oceans toward it.

Highs and lows

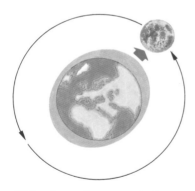

Tides rise as the moon circles Earth. The gravity of the moon tugs at the oceans, pulling the water around with it.

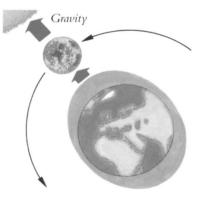

Gravity

Once every two weeks, the sun and the moon line up with Earth. Their combined pull creates a spring tide.

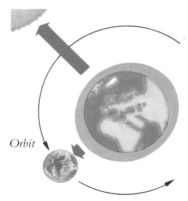

Orbit

One week later, the sun and the moon are at right angles to each other. Their pull is in different directions, creating a neap tide.

High tide

At high tide, these sailboats *(above)* are floating in the water. The sea has reached its highest point on the shore.

Low tide

About six hours ago, these sailboats *(below)* were floating in the water. Now the tide has gone out, leaving the boats high and dry at low tide.

Beating the flood

The Thames tidal barrier, on the outskirts of London, England, is designed to protect parts of inner London from flooding that could occur if exceptionally high tides, driven by gale-force winds, swept up the River Thames from its estuary. The tidal barrier extends 569 yards (520.3 m) across the Thames and has ten movable steel gates under the riverbed. The gates are raised to form the barrier when danger threatens.

OCEAN EDGE

THE sea is often the most awesome at the ocean's edge where it attacks the land and changes the landscape. Seawater pounds the shore like a battering ram, and the sand particles it carries act like a grindstone as they erode earth and rock. Waves force air into cracks in the rocks, widening the cracks and, eventually, breaking up the rock face. New land is also created at the ocean's edge as great rivers drop their sediment — loads of mud, rock, and sand. When the amount of sediment is too much for the sea to carry away, a muddy plain, called a delta, forms. Sometimes, large deposits of sediment accumulate at the river's mouth, and the river is forced to branch out into smaller streams to flow around them. These branches form a delta shaped like a bird's foot.

At its mouth, the River Torridge (above) in southwestern England drops its load of mud and pebbles and changes course.

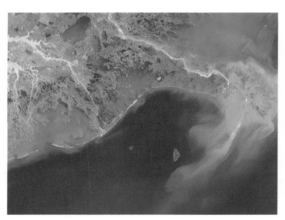

Bird-foot delta
This view from space shows how the Mississippi River has dropped its sediment to form a huge, bird-foot delta. Plumes of light-colored sediment spill out into the Gulf of Mexico.

A riverboat chugs down the Mississippi River in Louisiana. The color of the water shows that this river carries vast quantities of mud. This mud will become part of the Mississippi delta.

Sea caves and arches

In Normandy, France, the soft chalky cliffs are continually being eroded, or worn away, by the relentless attack of the sea. Some parts of the cliffs are made from softer rock than the rest. These rocks are eroded more quickly by battering waves. In this coastal scene *(below)*, caves have been carved out of the bottom of cliffs in some places, and arches have been sculpted just offshore. Bays are created the same way — by the sea pounding onto softer rocks. Harder rocks resist erosion and form headlands that jut into the sea.

FACT BOX

• One of the world's first great civilizations developed on the Nile River delta in Egypt. Annual flooding along the banks of the river kept the soil fertile, so it was very good for growing crops.

• In stormy weather, powerful waves can batter cliffs along the coast by hurling rocks weighing over 100 pounds (45 kilograms) 30 yards (27 m) or more through the air.

Black sandcastles

Sand is a feature of many seashores. On Lanzarote *(above)*, one of the Canary Islands, the beaches are black. The island has a volcanic origin, which means it formed from molten rock that rose from the ocean floor. Ordinary sand is made up of tiny grains of light-colored rock, seashells, and coral. Volcanic sand consists of minute grains of dark volcanic rock called basalt.

THE CHANGING COASTLINE

You will need:
sand, plastic bucket, measuring cup
or pitcher of water, water tank.

THE great rivers of the world remove millions of tons of mud, rock, and sand from the land every day and carry them into the sea. The flowing water cuts its way through deeply at first. Then, as the river loses speed, it divides into many channels. When the water slows down, it drops what it is carrying as sediment. After a while, this sediment takes on the shape of a fan, or delta. The project on the opposite page shows how to copy this natural process and make your own delta. In delta regions, the land is gradually advancing into the sea. Elsewhere, the opposite is happening — the sea is advancing into the land, as its waves wear away the coastline. The project on this page shows how waves erode the land. Although seawalls often are built to protect the land, the power of waves is very difficult to withstand.

Make waves

1 Mix a little water with sand in a bucket until the sand is quite wet and sticks together firmly. Pack the sand in a wedge shape at one end of the tank.

2 Pour water into the empty end of the tank — carefully, so it doesn't disturb the sand too much. Fill the tank until the water covers about two-thirds of the sloping sand.

3 Make gentle waves in the water opposite the sand. Notice how the waves gradually wear away the slope. The same thing happens to sand on a seashore.

Make a delta

1 Trim a cardboard box so it is 5 to 6 inches (12.5 to 15 cm) deep. Use trash can liners to make the box waterproof.

2 Line the inside of the box and tape the plastic securely at each end. Make sure the seal between the liners is tight.

3 Use a trowel to spread sand about 2 inches (5 cm) deep over the bottom of the tray. Flatten and smooth the sand with the trowel.

4 Rest one end of the box on a block of wood to make a slope. Pour water onto the sand in the middle of the high end of the slope.

MATERIALS

You will need: scissors, long cardboard box, 2 plastic trash can liners, tape, trowel, sand, block of wood, measuring cup or pitcher of water.

As you continue pouring, you will find that the water gradually makes a path through the sand and deposits the sand it has carried away at the low end of the slope, in a delta region.

ISLANDS

MANY islands are scattered across the oceans. Some islands, called continental islands, stand in shallow seas and, at one time, were joined to continents. For example, Greenland was once joined to North America, and the British Isles were once part of mainland Europe. Some islands, called land-tied islands, are very close to shore and are tied to the shore by a sandbar, like a causeway. Other islands lie in the middle of the oceans, far away from any continents. These oceanic islands were formed by volcanic action occurring over many years. Some, such as the Hawaiian Islands, grew up over volcanic hot spots in Earth's crust. Others, such as Iceland, lie in regions where volcanic activity is taking place along plate boundaries.

This coral garden in the Solomon Islands in the Pacific Ocean has many different kinds of corals. Corals are beautiful, but they have hundreds of stinging tentacles to kill their prey.

How a coral atoll develops
Coral often grows in the shallow waters around a volcanic island.

As the island sinks or the sea rises, the coral continues to grow.

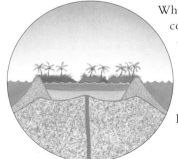

When the island completely disappears, a ring of coral, called a coral atoll, remains around a lagoon.

Coral circle
Circular atolls, or coral islands, are found in spots throughout the warm Indian and Pacific oceans. They first grow up around a volcanic island, then continue growing as the island gradually sinks into the sea.

Tied to the land

Mont St. Michel, an island close to the coast of Brittany in northwestern France, is a classic example of a land-tied island. Land-tied islands are offshore islands connected to the shore by a sandbar that has been deposited by ocean currents. Mont St. Michel is joined to the mainland by a raised road, or causeway, about 1 mile (1.6 km) long.

Hot and cold

Many hot springs, like this one *(above)*, are found in Iceland. Iceland is a volcanic island located where the Mid-Atlantic Ridge rises to the surface of the sea. Water, heated by hot rock underground, bubbles to the surface as hot springs.

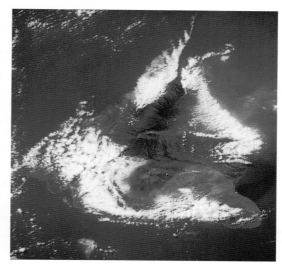

Big smoky

On the Big Island of Hawaii, smoke pours out of erupting volcanoes. All of the Hawaiian Islands are tips of underwater volcanoes that erupted on the ocean floor and rose to the surface.

LIFE IN THE OCEANS

L IFE on Earth began in the oceans about three billion years ago. It took a long time, however, before organisms like those found today made their first appearance. Traces of them can be found in rocks about 600 million years old. They include simple animals, such as jellyfish and worms. Today, the seas contain millions of different species of animals. Almost all of them ultimately depend on simple plants, called phytoplankton, for their food. Phytoplankton float in seawater where tiny animals, called zooplankton, graze on them. Larger animals eat the zooplankton and are then eaten themselves by still larger animals. Each animal is a link in what is known as a food chain.

Ocean pyramid
This food pyramid shows the feeding relationships in an ocean food chain. Simple plants, called phytoplankton, are eaten in large amounts by zooplankton. The tiny zooplankton are then eaten by the next level in the chain, herrings, which, in turn, are eaten by cod. Finally, porpoises eat the cod.

porpoise

cod

herring

zoo-plankton

phytoplankton

Animal tree
This illustration *(right)* shows the main animal groups that live in the sea, from simple single-celled protozoa to vertebrates, or larger backboned fish and mammals. These groups are arranged in the shape of a tree, with each group shown on a different branch.

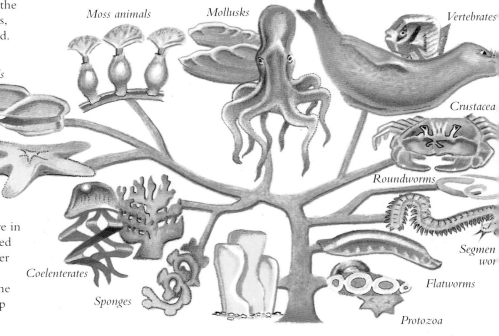

Moss animals

Mollusks

Vertebrates

Brachiopods

Crustacea

Echinoderms

Roundworms

Coelenterates

Segmented worms

Sponges

Flatworms

Protozoa

Microscopic zooplankton (above) *are near the bottom of the ocean food chain. They feed on equally small plant life called phytoplankton, which are tiny floating algae.*

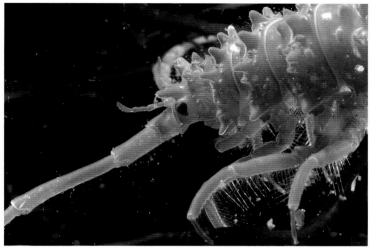

Tiny crustaceans
Tiny crustaceans live in huge numbers in the oceans. Many of them are krill *(above)*, tiny shrimplike creatures that are the main food for most baleen whales.

Open wide
These humpback whales are feeding. You can see their plates of baleen, which they use to filter small creatures from the seawater. Humpbacks also eat small fish, such as herring. Whales are at the top of the food chain because their only natural enemies are human beings.

SHORE LIFE

THE seashore is a challenging habitat for living things. It is constantly pounded by waves, exposed to salt spray, and alternately covered and uncovered by tides. Still, a remarkable number of animals and plants live in this habitat. The kinds of species found depend on the type of shore. Seaweed is a feature of rocky shores, where it attaches itself to the rocks. Seaweed is a type of algae, the simplest kind of plant life. Many crabs and mollusks, such as limpets and whelks, also live on rocky shores. Crabs and a few mollusks, such as clams, live on sandy shores, too, but the main residents of sandy shores live beneath the surface and include many kinds of worms.

Well-drilled
Dog whelks *(above)* prey on barnacles. The whelk bores through the shell of the barnacle to get at the soft body inside.

FACT BOX

• Seaweed called Pacific giant kelp can grow as much as 18 inches (45 cm) in a day and can eventually reach a length of 195 feet (60 m).

• Mollusks cause erosion by digging little pits in the rocks as they feed on seaweed.

• Seaweed was, for many years, the main source of the element iodine.

Mangroves, like these (above) *in the Florida Everglades, grow at the ocean's edge in tropical regions. As they grow, they send down roots from their branches, eventually forming a tangled thicket. These thickets are home to creatures such as mudskippers, a type of fish.*

Mudskippers

This mudskipper *(left)* is crossing the muddy surface of a mangrove swamp. Mudskippers get their name from their habit of skipping across mud, using their front fins as legs and flicking their tails. These remarkable creatures are fish that not only can walk but also can breathe air out of water.

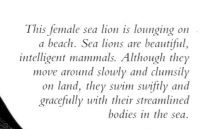

This female sea lion is lounging on a beach. Sea lions are beautiful, intelligent mammals. Although they move around slowly and clumsily on land, they swim swiftly and gracefully with their streamlined bodies in the sea.

Scurrying scavengers

These crabs *(above)* are scavenging for food on a shore of the Galápagos Islands. Crabs are crustaceans with soft bodies protected by hard shells. They have five pairs of jointed legs. The front pair of legs has strong pincerlike claws used to grasp prey. More than 4,500 species of crabs can be found throughout the world.

ON THE SHORE

For a nature detective, the seashore is a fascinating place. Whether the shore is sandy, muddy, pebbly, or rocky, it usually teems with life. Creatures can be found scurrying on the surface, hiding under rocks in tidepools, or burrowing in the sand. The shore also reveals many signs of previous life. On most shores, for example, you will find crab claws, cuttlefish bones, and all kinds of shells, such as those of clams, mussels, limpets, barnacles, and many snail-like creatures. Each of these creatures has a different kind of shell, grown to protect its soft body. In one of the projects on these two pages, you can discover how lovely shells are on the inside, as well as on the outside. You will also find out that shells are made of calcium carbonate, a chemical that shellfish take from the sea as they grow.

M A T E R I A L S

You will need: plastic bucket, fishing net, spade, magnifying glass, field guide, binoculars, notebook, pencil.

A search for life

1 On most seashores, you will find plenty of shells. See how many different kinds you can find and identify. Make sure the shells are empty before you take them.

2 You can find many kinds of living shells on the rocks. The one in the middle *(above)* is a limpet, which clings very strongly to rocks to avoid being swept out to sea.

3 You can often find creatures hiding under loose rocks in tidepools. Always replace the rocks to avoid damaging the habitat and harming the animals that live there.

4 Crabs are among the most common animals found in tidepools. Hold them across the back of their shells so they will not be able to nip you.

5 Many kinds of worms live in shore sand. They burrow deep, leaving holes when the tide goes out. Dig down to find the holes. Do you know which worms made them?

6 When you return from the seashore, take a closer look at the objects you have collected. Use field guides to help you identify the shells, seaweed, and small bones.

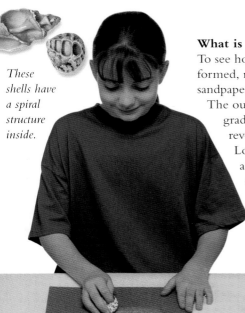

These shells have a spiral structure inside.

What is inside a shell?
To see how different shells are formed, rub them on coarse sandpaper or with a metal file. The outside layers will gradually wear away to reveal the structure inside. Look for shells with a beautiful spiral structure inside.

The acid test
To find out what shells are made of, scrape one with a file and collect the powder in a plastic lid. Adding vinegar to the powder will make it fizz, which tells you the shell is made of calcium carbonate. Acid in the vinegar acts on the alkaline carbonate, producing carbon dioxide.

SEABIRDS

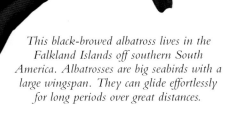

THE sea cliffs and shores provide a storehouse of food for bird life. Shoals of fish live in the surface waters, and burrowing worms, mollusks, and crustaceans inhabit the shores and nearby marshes and mudflats. Seabirds, such as albatrosses and shearwaters, spend most of their life at sea. They return to land only to breed. Gulls, cormorants, and puffins stay in coastal waters and are often seen on or near the shore. Other shorebirds are waders that look for food at the water's edge. These birds include avocets, oystercatchers, and sandpipers. In winter, vast flocks of migrating birds visit seaside habitats to escape from the cold elsewhere. Huge numbers of graylag and barnacle geese spend the winter on the estuary mudflats and saltwater marshes around the coasts of Britain.

This black-browed albatross lives in the Falkland Islands off southern South America. Albatrosses are big seabirds with a large wingspan. They can glide effortlessly for long periods over great distances.

Crowd trouble
Atlantic gannets crowded together at a nesting site squabble frequently. There is often a shortage of nesting sites on shore.

FACT BOX

• The arctic tern holds the world record for long-distance travel. It migrates some 21,700 miles (34,900 km) each year between the Arctic and the Antarctic.

• Gannets fish by diving into the water from heights of up to 90 feet (27 m).

• Cormorants dive as deep as 160 feet (49 m) below the surface when hunting for fish.

• The wingspan of a wandering albatross is the biggest of any bird — 11 feet (3.4 m).

• The male emperor penguin incubates the single egg laid by its mate by tucking it under a flap of skin on its abdomen.

This puffin (right) is enjoying a catch of tasty fish. Puffins have large bills that become very colorful during the breeding season. The female puffin lays her eggs in burrows dug into cliff tops.

Sifting mud

The avocet is one of the larger and more beautiful wading birds. It has long legs for wading and a long bill that curves at the end for sifting through mud to find small aquatic animals. Its unusual bill and striking black-and-white plumage make it easy to recognize.

Gentoo penguins dive into the sea in Antarctica. Penguins have a streamlined body for swimming. They have been known to reach speeds of up to 25 miles (40 km) per hour in the water, using their flipper-shaped wings as paddles.

WATCHING THE BIRDS

M A T E R I A L S

You will need: 6 long and 8 short bamboo canes, twine, large sheet of sand-colored fabric, safety pins, binoculars.

At the seaside, you will find two main groups of birds — true seabirds, such as gulls, and waders, such as sanderlings. Seabirds have short legs and webbed feet, used for swimming. You will often see them over the water diving for food. In general, they have strong, sharp bills, or beaks, for grasping and tearing at the fish they catch. Waders are quite different. Their feet are not webbed, and they usually have long legs for wading in the water. You will see them near the water's edge, particularly on the marshes and mudflats at the mouth of a river. They use their long bills to probe the sand and mud for food. One way to identify birds is by their plumage, or covering of feathers. Looking at their legs, feet, and bills will tell you a lot about them, too. Try to get as close to the birds as you can when you go bird-watching. If you camouflage yourself and stay very quiet, the birds will not notice you.

Build a blind

1 In a place on shore above the high tide level, push four long canes into the sand forming a square. Use twine to tie short canes between the long ones, top and bottom.

2 To make the frame stronger, tie two long canes diagonally across two opposite sides; for example, from the bottom left corner to the top right corner.

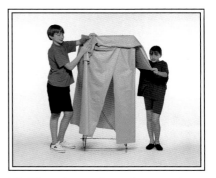

3 Then drape a large sheet or piece of fabric over the bamboo frame and tie it securely at the corners, both top and bottom, with twine. The blind is almost complete.

Tracking birds

To identify birds that have left tracks in the mud or sand on the shore, lay a sheet of acetate, or clear plastic, over the tracks and trace them. At home, copy the tracks into a notebook and use a field guide to identify them.

The sanderling is one of the most common shorebirds. Its tracks look quite different from those of other waders because, unlike most other small waders, it does not have a rear toe. It has only three toes, all pointing forward.

4 Use safety pins to fasten the edges of the sheet together. Leave openings between the pins to look through when you are watching the birds.

5 You will be able to see birds that come close to the blind with just your eyes, but you might want some binoculars handy to see birds that are farther away.

LIFE IN THE OPEN SEA

Marlins can leap high out of the water. The long "spear" on their mouths can be seen clearly. The spear is probably used when hunting prey.

THE surface waters of most oceans are light and relatively warm. As you go deeper, the water gets darker and colder, and the pressure increases rapidly. Marine life flourishes in the upper 650 feet (200 m) of these oceans, in the sunlight zone. This zone is where plankton thrive and support the ocean food chains. Jellyfish, shrimp, and fish such as herring and tuna all can be found here. These fish are eaten by predators, such as barracudas and sharks. Farther down, in the dimly lit twilight zone, are squid and octopus. No light at all can reach depths below 3,280 feet (1,000 m), yet life still exists. Strange-looking fish, such as viperfish with fierce inward-curving teeth and anglerfish with glowing "light bulbs" to lure their prey, live at these dark depths. Finally, worms and shrimplike creatures feed on the seabed.

FACT BOX

• Some squid escape their enemies by squirting brownish-black ink at them.

• The giant squid is the world's largest invertebrate, or animal without a backbone. It can grow to be over 40 feet (12 m) long.

• The ocean sunfish produces up to thirty million eggs when it spawns. Each egg has a diameter just over 1/16 inch (1.5 millimeters).

• The largest fish is the whale shark. It can grow to be over 40 feet (12 m) long and can weigh up to 15 tons (13.6 metric tons).

• The sailfish, with speeds of up to 43 miles (69 km) per hour, is probably the fastest fish.

Using their very large fins as wings, flying fish can glide through the air above the waves for distances of 96 feet (29 m) or more. The fish launches itself into the air with a flick of its strong tail. Flying fish live in warm tropical regions around the world.

A deep-sea anglerfish has a "light" above its head and a huge mouth with big teeth. This anglerfish (right) changed color after it was caught. Normally, it is as pitch-black as the sea that surrounds it. Its "light" comes from light-producing organs, called esca. In some species, the light is much longer than the fish's body. The light attracts other fish for the angler to gobble up. Although they look fierce, most deep-sea anglerfish are small enough to fit in the palm of your hand.

The octopus is named for its eight tentacles. Each tentacle has one or two rows of sucker discs, used to handle prey when hunting and feeding. Tentacles are also used for moving around on the seabed. The octopus swims by water-jet propulsion, squirting water out of an opening, called a siphon, in its head.

The razor-sharp teeth of the great white shark are deadly. They can cut through flesh with ease. Most sharks have several rows of teeth, which are shed and replaced row by row. Although the great white shark is famous for being extremely dangerous to humans, it usually feeds on fish, turtles, and seals.

SEA MAMMALS

Bottle-nosed dolphins adapt well to human companionship and can be trained easily.

THE most advanced group of animals on Earth are the mammals. They are warm-blooded and breathe air. Most female mammals give birth to live young and produce milk in their bodies to feed them. Mammals live mainly on land, but some thrive in the sea, including whales, the largest mammals of all. Dolphins, porpoises, seals, and sea lions are sea mammals, too. They all are well adapted to a watery habitat. Sea mammals have an insulating layer of fatty tissue, called blubber, under their skin to keep out the cold. All sea mammals swim fast and gracefully. The killer whale, which is actually a dolphin, can reach speeds of up to 31 miles (50 km) per hour. On land, seals and sea lions slide and wriggle. They find climbing difficult, but they can move nimbly over a rocky shore.

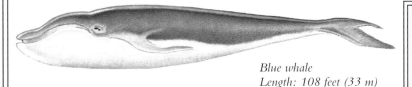

Blue whale
Length: 108 feet (33 m)

Killer whale
Length: 25 feet (8 m)

Human diver
Height: 6 feet (1.8 m)

African elephant
Height: 11 feet (3.4 m)

The blue whale is the largest animal ever to live. It can grow to be over 108 feet (33 m) long and can weigh up to 150 tons (136 metric tons), bigger than the largest dinosaur and as long as a line of six or more elephants. Except for the fact that the blue whale's body is supported by water, its weight would crush its internal organs.

FACT BOX

• Humpback whales blow bubbles as they swim in a spiral under a school of fish. The frightened fish start swimming very close together. Then, the whale, with its mouth wide open, surfaces in the middle of the fish and swallows them.

• The sperm whale can dive to depths of 9,840 feet (3,000 m) to find food. It can stay underwater for two hours before coming up to the surface to breathe.

• The humpback whale communicates over distances of more than 62 miles (100 km) by singing a unique song. The song can last up to thirty minutes.

To breach, or leap, out of the water, a humpback whale speeds forward through the water and then flicks its powerful tail, which takes it up to, and above, the surface. For an animal weighing tens of tons, breaching is a remarkable feat. No one knows why whales breach. It is probably a way of communicating. The loud splash can be heard many miles (km) away.

A killer whale surges toward shore hunting elephant seals. The killer whale is one of the few whales that comes to shore on purpose. In some regions, such as the Crozet Islands in the Indian Ocean, killer whales swim right onto the beach to prey on baby sea lions.

A monk seal swims gracefully in Hawaiian waters, using its flippers as paddles. Its body is streamlined, so it can glide easily through the water.

LIFE ON A CORAL REEF

CORAL reefs are found in tropical and subtropical regions of the world. The tiny animals that build them can exist only if the water is more than 64°F (18°C). Coral is built by tiny, jellylike animals called polyps. As they grow, polyps extract calcium from the sea and deposit it as hard, limy cups around their bodies. When they die, other polyps grow on their limy remains, and, slowly, a reef builds up. Coral reefs are one of the oceans' richest habitats. They provide plenty of food and shelter for a host of different species — sea anemones, sponges, starfish, giant clams that grow up to 3½ feet (1 m) wide, an abundance of colorful fish, and vicious moray eels on the prowl for food. Some animals, such as parrot fish, eat coral and severely damage the reefs.

This coral is found in the Red Sea, which lies between Africa and the Arabian peninsula. The Red Sea is famous for the colorful coral reefs that thrive in the warm waters of that region.

FACT BOX

• Australia's Great Barrier Reef is about 1,240 miles (1,995 km) long and covers over 77,200 square miles (200,000 sq km).

• The crown–of–thorns starfish eats coral and can devastate reefs. The Great Barrier Reef is badly affected by this creature.

• Most coral reefs are found in warm waters between the Tropic of Cancer in the Northern Hemisphere and the Tropic of Capricorn in the Southern Hemisphere.

• Starfish are not fish. They are creatures called echinoderms, which means they have spiny skin. Most starfish have five arms and hundreds, or even thousands, of tube feet.

Safety in numbers

A school of fish called antheas stay close to their coral reef home. These small fish would be easy targets for larger predators if they swam alone. Together, however, they confuse their attackers, which is why many species of fish swim in schools.

A moray eel, one of the most feared predators in coral reefs, has a large mouth and powerful teeth for catching prey. Some species can grow up to 10 feet (3 m) long.

The hinged shell of this giant clam (above), on a coral reef at Heron Island, Australia, could weigh as much as a quarter of a ton.

A clown fish (right) can nestle among the stinging tentacles of a sea anemone. No predators dare come near for fear of being stung. The clown fish is quite safe, and the anemone benefits by picking up food scraps that the clown fish drops. This kind of two-way partnership between different species is called symbiosis.

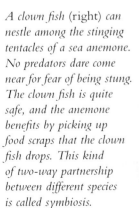

SHIPS

Ships have been sailing the oceans for at least five thousand years. Today, merchant ships are still the main means for transporting goods and materials overseas. Most ships used to be made of wood and powered by wind caught in their sails. Most ships now are made from steel plates welded together, and they are powered by diesel engines or steam turbines. Cruise ships do not look like merchant ships. They have cabins, shops, and restaurants high above main deck level. This raised part of a ship is called the superstructure. Bulk carriers, such as oil tankers, have very little superstructure. They carry their cargo in large tanks, or holds, below deck.

Tall ships
These ships *(above)* have gathered in a harbor in Sweden to celebrate the golden age of sailing (mid-1800s). The two large square-riggers are training ships for sailors.

A flotilla, or small fleet, of tugboats (left) is towing an oil rig down a river in Louisiana to the sea. Tugs are small, tough, and powerful boats that are easy to handle in difficult conditions.

FACT BOX

• The *Norway* is the longest passenger liner ever built — over 1,000 feet (300 m) long. The *Norway* was built in 1960.

• Clippers were the swiftest sailing ships. They were built in the 1800s to carry goods between the Far East and the Americas.

• In 1992, the powerboat *Destriero* made the fastest crossing of the Atlantic — 2 days, 10 hours, and 35 minutes.

Twin hulls

A catamaran ferry *(right)* transports passengers quickly and comfortably. It has two slim hulls instead of a single broad hull like a normal boat. With less hull in the water, the catamaran has less drag, which means it can travel much faster than a normal boat.

Handy containers

This ship *(left)* has containers piled high on its deck. Although they might be filled with a variety of cargo, the containers are always the same size so they can be loaded easily onto trucks and trains.

Skimming the waves

A hydrofoil passenger ferry *(right)* travels at high speeds. Hydrofoils have underwater wings, called foils, that lift the hull, or main body, of the ship out of the water. The faster the speed, the greater the lift as the ship skims over the water.

FLOATING AND HOVERING

M A T E R I A L S

You will need: scissors, colored paper, plastic drinking straw, tape, modeling clay, water tank.

U NTIL early in the nineteenth century, ships were made of wood, because wood is lighter than water and floats on top of it. Most ships today, however, are made of steel, which is much heavier than water. Some ships, such as aircraft carriers and tankers, weigh hundreds of thousands of tons. How can they float? They float because of upthrust, a force in the water that holds things up. Anything will float if the upthrust is greater than its weight. Upthrust is the basic principle behind ship design. The project on this page shows how a broad hull increases the upthrust on a ship and allows it to float. Some sea vessels do not float — they hover. Gliding on a cushion of air above the water, they can travel very fast.

Which will float — a solid ball or a hollowed-out bowl of modeling clay?

Ship shaping

3 Reshape the modeling clay to look like a bowl and stick the sail back in it. This time the ship will float in the tank of water.

1 To make a ship, cut out a triangle of colored paper for a sail and tape a straw to the middle of it. Then roll some modeling clay into a ball and stick the sail in it.

2 Fill a tank with water and put the ship in it. It will sink immediately, like a stone. Building a ship out of solid heavy material does not work!

You will need: a brick, plastic bag, hanging scale, notebook, pencil, water tank.

Hovering

Turn a cold glass upside down on a wet tray and push it with your finger. It will not move much. Dip the glass in hot water from the tap and try again. The glass will slide around easily because hot air is escaping around the bottom. The glass is hovering like a hovercraft.

Measuring upthrust

1 Place a brick in a plastic bag and hang it from the hanging scale. Watch where the pointer stops on the scale and write down this weight in a notebook.

2 Weigh the brick again, but, this time, lower it into a tank of water until it is submerged. The weight will be less than before because of upthrust on the brick.

This hovercraft ferry is crossing the English Channel, gliding along on a cushion of air.

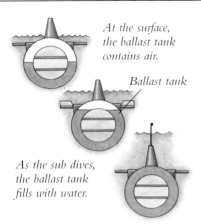

At the surface, the ballast tank contains air.

Ballast tank

As the sub dives, the ballast tank fills with water.

When the submarine is submerged, the ballast tank is full of water.

Ballast tanks

Submarines dive by filling their ballast tanks with water. To surface, they release water from the ballast tanks and replace it with air.

SUBMARINES

SUBMARINES travel silently beneath the surface of the water. Most of them are naval vessels, and they are quite different from surface ships. Submarines are built for military use. They are designed to sneak up on targets without being seen. A submarine has an enclosed hull that is smooth and streamlined to slip through the water easily. It has a small, raised superstructure, called the conning tower, which houses the bridge used for navigation and other operations. When the submarine is shallowly submerged, a periscope can be used to see things above the surface of the water. A submarine dives and surfaces by letting water into and pumping water out of ballast tanks. Smaller civilian submarines, called submersibles, are used for deep-sea research work and to assist in diving operations.

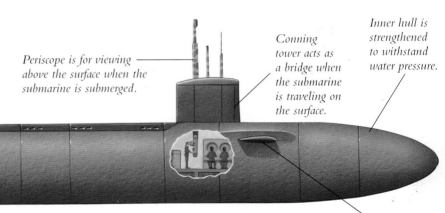

Propeller spins to drive the submarine.

Engine room contains turbines that spin the propeller shaft.

Periscope is for viewing above the surface when the submarine is submerged.

Conning tower acts as a bridge when the submarine is traveling on the surface.

Inner hull is strengthened to withstand water pressure.

Rudder helps steer the submarine.

Rear diving plane can be angled up or down to make the submarine surface or dive.

Forward diving plane

Fast and deadly

The main parts of a submarine are the propeller, the rudder, and the diving planes. The propeller provides propulsion, or power; the rudder is used for steering; and the diving planes are used for diving and surfacing.

Nuclear-powered

This U. S. Navy submarine *(left)* is powered by a nuclear reactor that heats water into steam in a boiler. The steam drives a turbine that spins the propeller. Nuclear submarines can stay submerged for months without surfacing.

Diving submersible

Mini-subs, called submersibles *(below)*, are used for scientific research, as well as for underwater salvage and construction. Usually, they have a crew of only two or three and dive for a day or less.

Deepest diver

The *Trieste,* a bathyscaphe, deep-diving vessel, made the deepest-ever ocean descent in 1960, diving into the Mariana Trench, in the Pacific Ocean, to a depth of 36,000 feet (10,973 m).

UP PERISCOPE

SUBMARINES can travel beneath the surface of the water to approach a target without being spotted, so they have periscopes that submarine commanders can use to see what is happening on the surface. A periscope gives the commander an all-around view of the surface while the submarine stays hidden underwater. A periscope has two mirrors that reflect light down a long tube into the commander's eye and a telescope that magnifies distant objects. It can move up and down as well as in a complete circle. When the submarine is underwater, observations can be made with just the tip of the periscope peeping out above the waves. This project shows how to make a periscope that you can use to look around corners and over walls without being seen.

MATERIALS

You will need: ruler, pencil, large piece of stiff cardboard, scissors, tape, 2 flat mirrors.

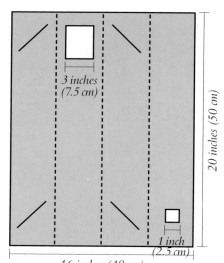

3 inches
(7.5 cm)

20 inches (50 cm)

1 inch
(2.5 cm)

16 inches (40 cm)

Use these measurements (above) to make a periscope.

Make a periscope

1 Divide a piece of cardboard into four equal sections *(as shown, left)*. Using the back of a scissors, carefully score along the dividing lines to make folding easier.

2 Cut out slots at 45° angles, for the mirrors, in two sections *(as shown, far left)*. Ask an adult to cut out an eyehole and a viewing window in the other two sections.

Zigzag light
Light enters a periscope through the window at the top and is reflected by the top mirror downward onto the bottom mirror. The bottom mirror, in turn, reflects the light through the eyehole and into the viewer's eye.

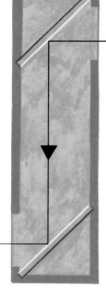

Periscope view
Below the surface, a submarine officer can see what is happening on the surface through a periscope. The black-and-white picture *(above, right)* is what the officer actually sees.

5 Your periscope is ready for action. You can use it to look over high walls and hedges and to peek around corners.

3 Fold the cardboard along the scoring to form a square tube. Tape the edges, inside and out. Cut out cardboard squares and tape them to the top and bottom of the tube.

4 Carefully push mirrors into the slots at the top and bottom of the tube. Tape them securely in place. Make sure the mirrors face out of the eyehole and viewing window.

DIVING

THE sea is not a natural habitat for humans, who need air to breathe and are used to an atmosphere that is light and warm. The sea is cold and, the deeper you go, the greater the pressure on your body from the weight of the water. Using modern equipment, divers can descend 160 feet (50 m), which is not particularly deep, but is a safe limit for air-breathing scuba divers. Scuba stands for Self-Contained Underwater Breathing Apparatus. To protect themselves from the cold, scuba divers usually wear close-fitting waterproof suits. Depending on the length or depth of the dive, a diver might wear an electrically heated suit. Breathing a special mix of gases, scuba divers can reach depths of 1,968 feet (600 m). Divers using special experimental chambers have reached depths of 3,280 feet (1,000 m).

Scuba diving
This diver *(above)* is exploring a shipwreck on the seabed. Scuba divers wear face masks and, through tubes, breathe air stored under pressure in tanks worn on their backs.

Shallow breathing
These children *(right)* are snorkeling. A snorkel fits over the mouth, and air for breathing comes through a pipe that sticks out of the water while the face is submerged underwater.

Pearls form inside the shells of pearl oysters, shellfish that live in tropical seas. A pearl forms as the oyster makes a coating around an irritating particle, such as a grain of sand, that enters its shell.

Pearl diving

This diver has been harvesting pearl oysters from the seabed off the coast of Australia. He is wearing a heavy diving suit so he can walk on the ocean bottom. Air pumped through a hose from a tank on board the boat is the diver's vital life-support system.

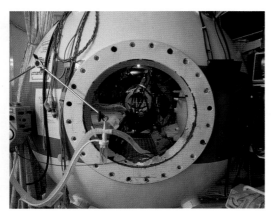

Under compression

Divers who work long periods of time at great depths rest in an underwater compression chamber *(left),* which helps them adjust to the lower surface pressure.

FACT BOX

• For every 33 feet (10 m) of depth, the pressure of seawater increases by 1 atmosphere (the pressure at the surface).

• When the bathyscaphe *Trieste* dived to 36,000 feet (10,973 m) in the Pacific Ocean, it had to withstand water pressure of more than a ton on every ½ square inch (3.2 square centimeters) of its hull.

• For deep dives, breathing a mixture of helium and oxygen prevents nitrogen narcosis, or the bends, a dangerous condition caused by excess nitrogen in the blood. This mixture makes divers' voices sound like Donald Duck's.

DIVE, DIVE, DIVE

PEOPLE were diving and working on the seabed long before there were protective diving suits. The earliest diving device used was called a diving bell. For deep dives, air under pressure is fed into diving bells to keep water out. After breathing air under pressure for a long time, divers who surface too quickly can suffer from the bends. When the pressure is released, gas in their blood bubbles out, causing muscle pain, paralysis, coma, or even death. Pressure is an important part of the projects featured on these two pages. When operating the diver in the project on the opposite page, squeezing the sides of the jar forces water into a small tube, compressing the air inside. With more water in it, the tube is less buoyant and sinks.

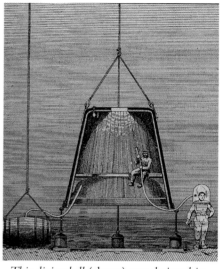

This diving bell (above) was designed in 1690 by scientist Sir Edmund Halley. Air from the bell was piped into a diver's helmet.

The diving bell
Turn a glass upside down and push it into a tank of water. Air trapped inside the glass keeps most of the water out. A diving bell works in much the same way, but, as the diver uses up air in the diving bell, more is pumped in.

The bends
Point a soft drink bottle away from your face and slowly unscrew the cap. Bubbles of gas appear. The gas was dissolved under pressure in the drink. When the pressure was released, the gas bubbled out. When divers rise to the surface too quickly, nitrogen in their blood bubbles out in a similar way, causing the bends.

Make a diver

1 Stick modeling clay around the outside of the mouth of a small tube, to weigh the tube down. You might have to add or remove some clay after the test in step 2.

2 Put the tube into an open jar of water. Let water into the tube, but leave a bubble of air at the top, so when you let it go, it floats. Add or remove clay, as needed.

3 When it is floating correctly, take the tube out of the water by covering its mouth with your thumb, while it is still underwater, and carefully lifting it out.

4 Transfer the tube to a plastic container filled with water to the very top. After you put the tube in the water, take your thumb away. Then screw the lid onto the jar.

M A T E R I A L S

You will need: modeling clay, small tube, large open jar of water, plastic container with lid.

5 Squeeze the sides of the container tightly. The tube will dive to the bottom because the pressure of squeezing forces water into it, making it less buoyant. If you stop squeezing, the tube will rise.

THE SEA'S RESOURCES

This net is bulging with fish. Fishermen haul in an estimated 80 million tons (72.6 million metric tons) of fish from the world's oceans each year. Overfishing, however, has led to shortages.

THE sea is vast and has abundant resources. The most obvious resource is fish. Fish have always been part of the human diet. They are rich in protein, oils, vitamins, and minerals. The sea also is a great storehouse of chemicals, including sodium, chlorine, magnesium, and bromine. Salt can be extracted by evaporating seawater in shallow salt pans. Many precious resources, such as oil and natural gas, lie hidden under the seabed, too. These fossil fuels are trapped in the rocks and can be extracted by drilling. The sea is potentially a major source of energy. Tidal power is already being used with some success, and there are plans to use the heat from warm waters to drive turbines.

These people are working in a salt pan in Thailand. In salt panning, seawater is collected in shallow basins or ponds along the coast. The heat of the sun gradually evaporates the seawater, leaving the salt behind.

Desalination plants provide drinking water in hot desert countries in the Middle East where water shortages occur. Desalination, or taking salt out, involves heating seawater until it boils. When the steam produced by the boiling is cooled, the water condenses as a pure liquid.

Fossil fuels

This gas rig *(left)* is in the North Sea. Most gas and oil wells are on a continental shelf in relatively shallow waters, such as the North Sea, the Caribbean, the Gulf of Mexico, and the Gulf of Guinea.

OTEC

The idea behind this design *(above)* for a massive floating energy plant, called OTEC (ocean thermal energy conversion), is to use the solar energy stored in surface waters of the ocean to produce electricity. The hot water is evaporated into a gas that drives turbines to generate electricity.

Tidal power

La Rance Tidal Power Station *(right),* near St. Malo in France, is the first of its kind. Tidal power uses the continual ebbing and flowing of tides as a power source to drive electricity generators.

SAVING THE SEAS

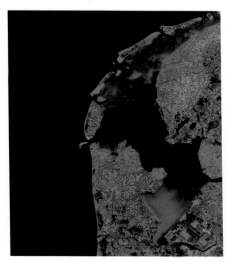

The Netherlands, shown in this satellite view (above), *is a low-lying country. Because air pollution is making Earth warmer, sea levels could rise, and the Netherlands could be completely flooded.*

People once thought the oceans were so big that whatever they did to them would make no difference. They dumped garbage into the sea and expanded fishing fleets to catch more fish and whales for food. Unfortunately, the oceans are not indestructible. Fish catches have dropped, and some whale species have come close to extinction. Serious oil tanker accidents have occurred, polluting beaches and killing marine life. Environmental groups throughout the world are now raising their voices in efforts to resolve some of these problems. Governments all over the world also are becoming more aware of these issues. Most countries have banned or restricted the killing of whales and have introduced fishing quotas to reduce the world's fish catches. Some marine habitats are being protected, and new techniques are being developed to cope with oil spills and pollution. These are only the first steps. Much more still needs to be done to protect the future of the oceans.

These workers are trying to cope with an oil tanker disaster in Alaska. The oil gets stickier the longer it sits, making it more difficult to remove and reducing the chances of survival for affected wildlife.

FACT BOX

• In the 1970s, tuna fishermen caught hundreds of thousands of dolphins in their nets every year. Now, most fishermen use nets with a specially designed fine-mesh panel that the dolphins can leap over to escape.

• Many marine species, from corals and giant clams to marine turtles and whales, are now protected by international organizations such as CITES, the Convention on International Trade in Endangered Species.

Great coral

Tourist planes are anchored off the Great Barrier Reef in northeastern Australia. It is the largest coral reef in the world, extending about 1,240 miles (1,995 km). Although the Reef has international protection as a world heritage site, tourism threatens it. Coral grows in shallow waters and can easily be damaged by tourist ships, amateur divers, and oil drilling.

Fish farms, like this one in a Scottish sea loch, do not conserve fish stocks in the open sea, but farmed fish do supplement the amount of fish available. As a result, salmon, trout, and oysters are not as rare as they used to be.

These tourists are watching whales feeding in Alaskan waters. Tours can help increase awareness that whales are still being slaughtered needlessly in some countries, threatening the extinction of many species.

GLOSSARY

algae – microscopic plants, with no roots, stems, or leaves, that cluster together by the millions and grow mostly in water and damp places.

atoll – an island of coral shaped like a ring surrounding a lagoon.

baleen – bonelike material that forms two rows of long plates in a whale's upper jaw, used to filter small animals, such as krill, out of the seawater for food.

ballast – something heavy in the bottom of a ship to make the ship steadier.

barnacle – a kind of crustacean that attaches itself to rocks, the hulls of ships, or larger marine animals and gathers food from the surrounding waters with its feathery appendages.

bathyscaphe – a watertight vessel, usually with a sphere-shaped cabin, that is able to navigate at great depths for ocean exploration.

bends – a dangerous illness, with chest and joint pains, convulsions, collapse, and possible paralysis, caused by bubbles of nitrogen in the bloodstream after leaving a compressed air atmosphere too quickly.

blind – a camouflaged enclosure in which to hide while watching birds or animals in their natural habitats.

bridge – the front part of the raised platform or enclosure (superstructure) on a ship, which usually houses the ship's navigation equipment.

buoyant – relatively light and able to float or rise in the air or when submerged in a liquid.

camouflage – to conceal, or hide, someone or something by disguising the person or object to blend in with the surroundings.

continental shelf – a shallowly submerged stretch of land around the edges of a continent that, at varying distances from shore, drops off in a steep slope to the ocean floor.

debris – remaining parts or pieces of things that have been broken down, discarded, or destroyed; rubbish.

estuary – a sea passage at the wide mouth of a river where the ocean's tide meets the river's current.

flotilla – a group, or fleet, of small boats working together under the same command toward a common goal.

habitat – the natural home of a plant or animal.

headland – a high and rocky piece of land that sticks out into the sea.

hull – the sides and bottom, or frame, on the main body of a large boat or ship.

hydrometer – a measuring instrument used to determine the density of a liquid.

krill – a type of zooplankton; tiny shrimplike crustaceans that are the main food of baleen whales.

limy – containing, covered with, or looking like lime or limestone.

mudflats – a level stretch of land just beneath the surface of the water that is covered and uncovered as tides move in and out.

neap tide – low tide, or tide with a minimum range.

organism – any living thing that needs a combination of physical organs to function; any kind of plant or animal life.

phytoplankton – microscopic plant organisms that float in water and make up the base level of the ocean food chain.

Plimsoll mark – a line on the side of a cargo ship to indicate the safe loading limit for a specific water condition.

seamount – an underwater mountain rising out of the seafloor.

sediment – matter carried and deposited by wind and water; matter that is suspended in a liquid and, when undisturbed, settles to the bottom.

shoals – large numbers gathered in groups, or schools; also, a shallow place in a body of water, especially over a sandbar.

spawn – to produce and deposit eggs in large numbers for reproduction, especially to reproduce aquatic animals.

spring tide – high tide, or tide with a maximum range.

subduction – the process in which one plate of Earth's crust slides under another, creating a deep trench where the plates meet.

submerge – to put under water (or another liquid); to plunge into water or cover with water.

submersible – able to be put into or covered with water (or another liquid).

symbiosis – two different kinds of organisms living in a close, cooperative relationship so that both will benefit.

tidepool – a pool of seawater that remains in a rocky hollow when the tide goes out (low tide) and contains a variety of hardy sea plants, such as algae, kelp, and sea lettuce, and simple animals, such as anemones, barnacles, crabs, and sponges.

tsunami – a huge tidal wave caused by an earthquake or volcanic eruption underwater.

upthrust – the upward push of water against objects placed in it; the force in the water that holds things up.

vessel – a large boat or ship, or some other craft bigger than a rowboat, that travels on water and carries cargo and passengers.

zooplankton – microscopic animal organisms that live in water, eat phytoplankton, and make up the second level of the ocean food chain, providing food for fish and larger marine animals.

BOOKS

Beneath Blue Waters: Meetings with Remarkable Deep-Sea Creatures. Deborah Kovacs and Kate Madin (Viking Penguin)

Coral Reefs. Lawrence Pringle (Simon and Schuster Children's)

Deep Sea Vents: Living Worlds Without Sun. John F. Waters (Dutton Children's Books)

Dying Oceans. Environment Alert! (series). Paula Hogan (Gareth Stevens)

The Incredible Coral Reef: Another Active-Learning Book for Kids. Toni Albert (Trickle Creek)

Islands. Robin Bates (Creative Education, Inc.)

Janice VanCleaves's Oceans for Every Kid: Easy Activities That Make Learning Science Fun. Science for Every Kid (series). Janice P. VanCleave (Wiley)

The Kelp Forest: The Ebb and Flow of Life in the Sea's Richest Habitat. Howard Hall (Silver Burdett)

Ocean Life. Under the Microscope (series). Casey Horton (Gareth Stevens)

Seas and Oceans. Nicola Barber (Trafalgar Square)

Submarines: Probing the Ocean Depths. Sean M. Grady (Lucent Books)

Tidepools: The Bright World of the Rocky Shoreline. Diana Barnhart and Vicki Leon (Silver Burdett)

VIDEOS

Creatures of the Blue. (IVN Communications, Inc.)

Junior Oceanographer. (Society for Visual Education, Inc.)

Life in the Sea (series). (National Geographic Educational Services)

Places in the Sea. (Journal Films, Inc.)

Scary, Slithery Creatures in the Water. (National Geographic Educational Services)

The Science of the Sea. (Journal Films, Inc.)

WEB SITES

www.hmu.auckland.ac.nz:8001/monz/seaweeding/index.html   octopus.gma.org/

Some web sites stay current longer than others. For further web sites, use your search engines to locate the following topics: *coastline, diving, islands, oceanography, oceans, saltwater, ships, submarines, tides, waves.*

INDEX

PICTURE CREDITS